WEATHER WATCH

Spring

by Cynthia Amoroso and Robert B. Noyed

Spring is here! Spring is one of the four **seasons**. It comes after winter and before summer.

Spring is the second season of the year.

In the spring, the cold days of winter are fading away. The sun shines longer during each day. It starts to get warmer outside.

This snow is melting from the warmer spring weather.

Spring days can be cloudy. Rain often falls from the clouds. The extra rain helps plants to grow.

Spring rain helps flowers grow.

The sunny days also help plants to grow. The leaves open on the trees. The grass turns green. Seeds begin to grow. Flowers start to **bloom**.

These plants are starting to grow in a garden.

Spring is a busy time for animals. Many animals give **birth** during this time of the year. Their babies welcome the warm sun.

A baby horse stands near its mother.

Many birds build their nests during the spring. They lay their eggs. Then baby birds **hatch** from the eggs.

A bird feeds its baby in a nest.

Spring is a busy time for people, too. Farmers plant seeds in their fields. Families enjoy the warm weather.

A farmer plants seeds in his field.

Children play outside in the spring. They ride their bikes. The windy days make it fun to fly kites.

A boy runs with a kite.

Spring is the time for baseball. Children get out their bats and balls. The nice weather makes people want to be outside.

These children are playing baseball.

Spring brings warm weather and sunshine. Look at the flowers and plants growing!

A garden is full of bright, colorful flowers.

Glossary

birth (BURTH): Birth is the event of something being born. Many animals give birth in the spring.

bloom (BLOOM): When flowers open up, they bloom. Many flowers bloom in the spring.

hatch (HACH): When baby animals come out of eggs, the eggs hatch. Many animals' eggs hatch in the spring.

seasons (SEE-zinz): Seasons are the four parts of the year. The four seasons are winter, spring, summer, and fall.

To Find Out More

Books

Branley, Franklyn M. *Sunshine Makes the Seasons*. New York: HarperCollins, 2005.

Lenski, Lois. *Spring Is Here*. New York: Random House, 2005.

Roca, Nuria. *Spring*. Hauppauge, NY: Barron's, 2004.

Web Sites

Visit our Web site for links about spring: *childsworld.com/links*

Note to Parents, Teachers, and Librarians: We routinely verify our Web links to make sure they are safe and active sites. So encourage your readers to check them out!

Index

About the Authors

Cynthia Amoroso has worked as an elementary school teacher and a high school English teacher. Writing children's books is another way for her to share her passion for the written word.

Robert B. Noyed has worked as a newspaper reporter and in the communications department for a Minnesota school district. He enjoys the challenge and accomplishment of writing children's books.

On the cover: Flowers are watered in a spring garden.

Published by The Child's World®
1980 Lookout Drive • Mankato, MN 56003-1705
800-599-READ • www.childsworld.com

ACKNOWLEDGMENTS
The Child's World®: Mary Berendes, Publishing Director
The Design Lab: Design and production
Red Line Editorial: Editorial direction

PHOTO CREDITS: Daniel Padavona/iStockphoto, cover; iStockphoto, cover, 3, 5, 9; Oscar Gutierrez/iStockphoto, 7; Hansjoerg Richter/iStockphoto, 11; Paul Tessier/iStockphoto, 13; Tom McNemar/iStockphoto, 15; Tatyana Chernyak/iStockphoto, 17; Melissa Carroll/iStockphoto, 19; Monika Lewandowska/iStockphoto, 21

Printed in the United States of America in Mankato, Minnesota.
July, 2010
PA02066

LIBRARY OF CONGRESS CATALOGING-IN-PUBLICATION DATA
Amoroso, Cynthia.
  Spring / by Cynthia Amoroso and Robert B. Noyed.
    p. cm. — (Weather watch)
  Includes index.
  ISBN 978-1-60253-363-9 (library bound : alk. paper)
  1. Spring—Juvenile literature. I. Noyed, Robert B. II. Title. III. Series.
  QB637.5.A46 2010
  508.2—dc22   2009030218